My Bible ALPHABET Book

A for Abraham to Z
for Zechariah in rhyme

Chariot Books™
David C. Cook Publishing Co.

A
is for Abraham
he was a friend of God.

You can read how Abraham was visited by the Lord in
Genesis 18:1–15.

B

is for Balaam
in evil paths he trod.

You can read how Balaam's donkey saw an angel in
Numbers 22:21–35.

C

is for Cornelius
to whom Peter help did bring.

You can read how Peter brought good news to the
Roman soldier, Cornelius, in
Acts 10:23–33.

D

is for David
he was Israel's royal king.

You can read how David was chosen as king in
I Samuel 16:4–13.

E
is for Elijah,
a prophet of the Lord.

You can read how Elijah was fed by ravens in
I Kings 17:1–6.

F

is for Felix
who trembled at the Word.

You can read how Paul preached to the Roman ruler, Felix, in
Acts 24:24–26.

G

is for Gideon,
the Midian hosts did beat.

You can read how Gideon beat the Midianite army in
Judges 7:1–25.

H

is for King Herod,
the wise men he did meet.

You can read how Herod sent the wise men to Bethlehem in
Matthew 2:1–8.

I

is for Isaac,
on an altar he was laid.

You can read how Abraham made an offering in
Genesis 22:1–14.

J

is for Jesus,
by Judas was betrayed.

You can read how Judas betrayed Jesus with a kiss in
Matthew 26:47–51.

On the cross He shed His blood
from sin to set us free,
Now life eternal through His name
is offered you and me.

You can read the story of Jesus' death on the cross in
Mark 15:25–30.

K
is for Keturah,
she was Abraham's second wife.

You can read about Abraham's family in
Genesis 25:1–4.

L

is for Lazarus,
whom Jesus raised to life.

You can read how Lazarus came out of his tomb in
John 11:38–44.

M

is for Moses,
by him the Law was given.

You can read how Moses received the Ten Commandments in
Exodus 20: 1–19.

N

is for Nicodemus,
whom Jesus taught the way to heaven.

You can read about Nicodemus' night time visit to Jesus in
John 3:1–3.

is for Obadiah,
who hid prophets in the caves.

You can read about Obadiah in
I Kings 18:1–6.

P
for Paul and Peter,
who taught us Jesus saves.

You can read the stories of Peter and Paul in the book of
Acts.

Q
is for Quartus,
friend of the apostle Paul.

We know from *Romans 16:23* that Quartus was a
Christian from Corinth.

R

is for Rachel,
Jacob loved her best of all.

You can read how Jacob married Rachel in
Genesis 29:14–30.

S

is for Stephen,
he was killed for preaching truth.

You can read about the death of Stephen in
Acts 6:8–14, 7:54–60.

T

is for Timothy,
trained in the Word from youth.

You can read how Timothy met the apostle Paul in
Acts 16:1–5.

U

is for Uriah,
by David's orders killed.

You can read how Uriah died in
II Samuel 11:14–17.

V

is for Queen Vashti,
the king with anger filled.

You can read how Queen Vashti made the king angry in
Esther 1:9–12.

W X AND Y

no matter where you look,
beginning with those letters
there are few names in God's Book.

Z
for Zechariah
in days of old did tell
the glorious coming of our Lord
as king on earth to dwell.

You can read Zechariah's prophecy in
Zechariah 9:9.

Now all that is written
in the pages of God's Book
is put there for our learning
as into it we look.